Collieries of Blae
& the Easter

John Cornwell

Landmark Publishing

——————— Published by ———————

The Oaks, Moor Farm Road West, Ashbourne, DE6 1HD
Tel: (01335) 347349
Fax: (01335) 347303
email: landmark@clara.net

1st Edition

13 ISBN: 978-1-84306-468-8

© **The late John Cornwell 2009**

The right of The late John Cornwell as author of this work has been asserted by his executor in accordance with the
Copyright, Design and Patents Act, 1993.

All rights reserved. No part of this publication may be reproduced, stored in a retrieval system or
transmitted in any form or by any means, electronic, mechanical, photocopying, recording or otherwise
without the prior permission of Landmark Publishing Ltd.

British Library Cataloguing in Publication Data: a catalogue record for this book is available
from the British Library.

Print: TJ International, Cornwall

Front Cover: Water Level at Blaenavon

Back Cover: Vivian Colliery, Abertillery around 1900

Page 1: Hafodyrynys mine. Electric locomotive at entrance to drift in 1968

Page 3: Marine Colliery. The unusual cast iron structure was made at the Risca Foundry Newport,
and appears to have been made from rising mains

Collieries of Blaenavon & the Eastern Valleys

John Cornwell

Landmark Publishing

CONTENTS

Featured Collieries

1 Blaenavon
2 Abertillery New Mine
3 Blaendare Drift Mine
4 Blaenserchan Colliery
5 Glyn Pits
6 Hafodyrynys Colliery and Mine
7 Llanhilleth Colliery
8 Marine Colliery
9 North Celynen and Graig Fawr Collieries
10 Six Bells Colliery
11 Tirpentwys Colliery

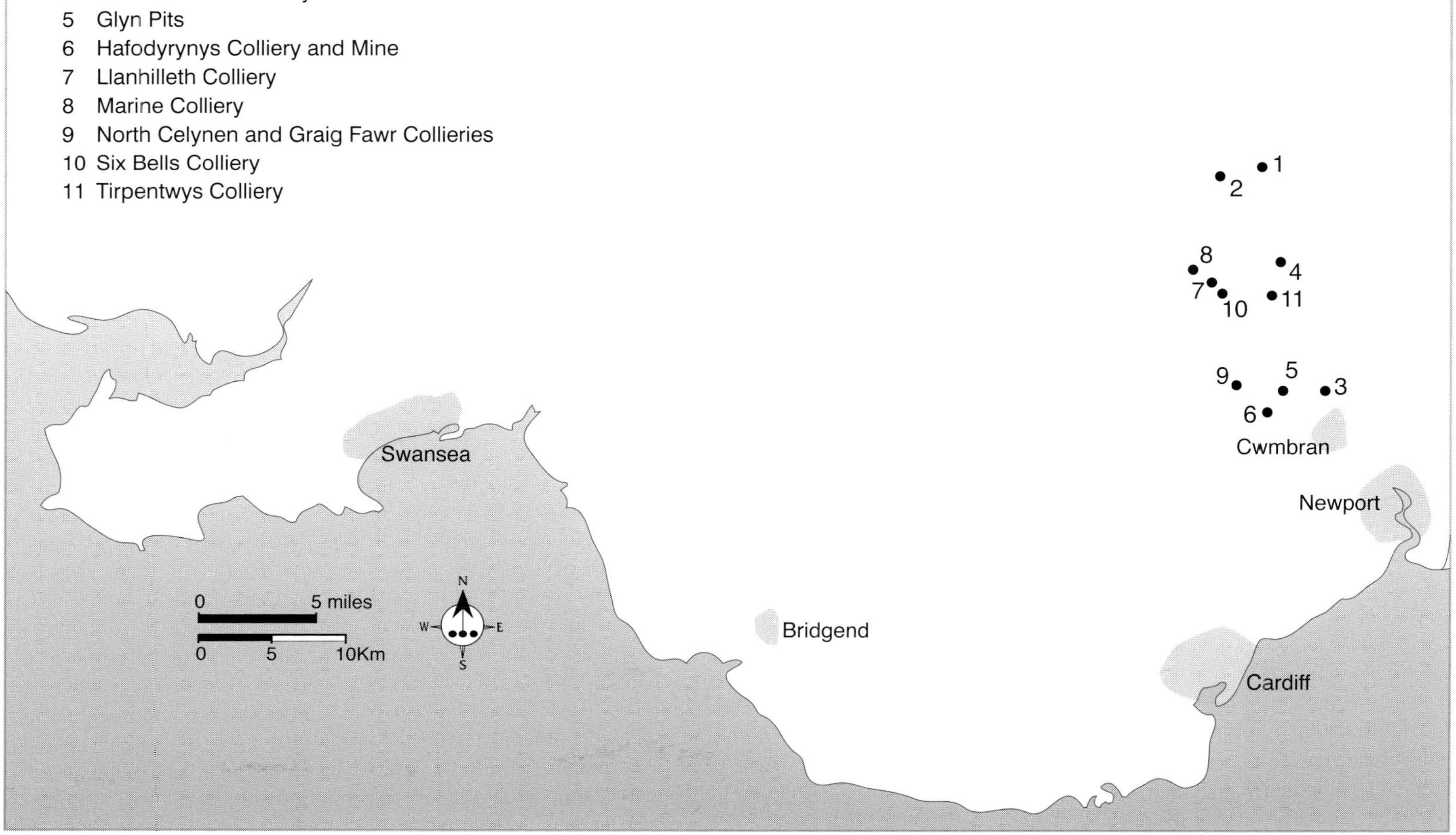
Swansea
Bridgend
Cwmbran
Newport
Cardiff
0 5 miles
0 5 10Km
N
W
E
S
1
2
3
4
5
6
7
8
9
10
11

INTRODUCTION

Nearly two decades have now elapsed since the closure of Deep Navigation Colliery, the last of the major colliery closures. This book records some of the more interesting and historical collieries and their workforce, that are now something of a distant memory.

In 1975 there were 47 working collieries and a number of colliery sites still maintained as pumping and ventilating units, like Tirpentwys, Clydach Merthyr, and many others. In the course of John Cornwall's work underground as a photographer recording the modern side of the industry, he was also allowed access on the surface and underground to record the historic buildings, machinery and underground workings of the South Wales Coalfield.

In the process of recording the industry he developed a technique of using the camera on a tripod with an open lens and using either a standard cap lamp or approved Locomotive lamp which had two batteries as opposed to one on a cap lamp. The lighting had to be approved as almost all photographs were taken in an atmosphere which normally contained firedamp, and flash was strictly forbidden. With this technique he developed a system of photographing shafts 1000ft deep, long lengths of roadways or portraits of men and objects sometimes only 3ft from the camera.

South Wales still has many interesting historical sites, despite the massive programme of clearance, some of which was not really necessary.

The object of this book is to place on record some of the history of the technology of the South Wales Coal field with its workforce. The book is not a definitive history, it is only a brief look into what was a large and very important industry which has almost disappeared.

Publisher's note: John Cornwell published his widely acclaimed book 'Collieries of South Wales Volume 1 & 2' in 2001 and 2002. His text has largely been left as he wrote it and therefore the reader is asked to note that some changes to surviving structures may have occurred since then.

The late John Cornwell

BLAENAVON COLLIERIES
Blaenavon, Monmouth

The first recorded working of coal in the Blaenavon area was in 1775, when William Tanner and Mary Gunter were granted a lease to work coal. The early workings were patch works and small levels situated on and around the extensive outcrop; many of these early sites still survive today to the north and west of Blaenavon.

It is probable that the first shaft to be sunk was the Engine Pit, which was sunk as a pumping pit. The sinking date is not known but would have been around 1800 to 1810; the Engine Pit Level would also have been driven about the same time.

The next major development would have been the sinking of the Cinder Pits, which are shown on the 1819 plan of Blaenavon, as intended Engine Pits for the deep work. The Cinder Pits were the scene of Blaenavon's worst mining disaster, on 28th November 1838 when torrential rain, after a heavy snowfall, ran off the hillsides and poured down the shafts of the Cinder Pits, drowning 14 men and two women.

Levels and collieries working before 1840:	
Aaron Brutes Level, c. 1800	Gain Pits, sunk around 1839
Black Pin Level, 1812	Gunter's Level
Bridge Level, 1782	Hill Pits, 1835
Cinder Pits, probable sinking 1819	Old Coal Pits
Dick Kear's Slope (New Slope), c. 1820	James Kearsley's Level
Engine Pit, 1800 to 1810	Old Slope
Engine Pit Level, 1800 to 1810	Parker's Level
Engine Coal Level, situated in the Iron Works yard	River Row Level
Forge Level, 1830?	Tunnel Level
Forge Pit	

After the erection of the New Furnaces at Forgeside by the Blaenavon Iron & Coal Co. in the 1840s, many new levels and pits were opened around the Forgeside Works:

Coity Pits, 1840	Forge Slope
Coity Level	Kearsley's Pit (later to be Big Pit)
Dodd's Slope, c. 1840	

Around 1878-79 Kearsley's Pit, which had been used as a ventilation shaft for the Forge Level and Pit, was deepened from the Threequarter seam depth of 128ft to the Old Coal at 293ft. The new colliery appeared in the Mines Inspectors' List of Mines as Big Pit in 1880, and by 1895 it was raising 5,000 tons of coal per week with Dodd's Slope.

Collieries Of The Blaenavon Iron & Steel Co. Ltd., 1900:

Colliery	Persons employed above ground	Persons employed below ground
Big Pit	370	200
Cinder Pits	Not worked since 1895	—
Dodd's Slope	179	26
Forge Slope	126	16
Gain Pits	149	17
Kay's Slope	328	54
Milfraen	199	23
Tunnel and Clay Level	35	6

Blaenavon Coal Seams:

Seam depth ft	Standard name	Local name	Thickness
76	Two Feet Nine	Elled	3ft 6in.
100	Upper Four Feet	Big Vein	3ft 0in.
127	Upper Six Feet	Threequarter	4ft 6in.
196	Upper Nine Feet	Horn or Top Rock	4ft 0in.
215	Nine Feet	Bottom Rock	5ft 6in.
224	Lower Nine Feet & Upper Bute	Black	
295	Yard	Meadow	3ft 6in.
311	Seven Feet	Yard	
370	Lower Five Feet & Gellideg	Old Coal	3ft 6in.
442	Garw	Garw & Engine Coal	2ft 6in.

BIG PIT, BLAENAVON, IN THE 1890s

Five of the seams were worked by the longwall system; the sixth, the Elled seam, was worke
on the pillar and stall method, horses being employed in hauling from the face workings
the bottom of the main road. From this point the trams were hauled by steam engine to th
pit bottom. There were four haulage engines in Big Pit supplied with steam from four Cornis
boilers. One engine in the Old Coal had two 18in. cylinders, and worked a haulage plain ov
3,600ft in length, with gradient of 1 in 12.

The original winding engine was constructed by Fowler Co. of Leeds. It had two 26in. ho
zontal cylinders and drums for flat ropes and could raise two trams in each cage.

Thirteen Cornish and egg-ended boilers supplied steam to the winding engine, and th
engines on Dodd's and Forge Slopes. The upcast shaft for Big Pit was the Coity Pit which ha
a Waddle fan.

Opposite page top: The two entrances of Dick Kears Slope in 1975, the blocked entrance is to the
left. The mine is shown on the 1883 O.S. map of the Blaenavon area

Opposite page bottom: Big Pit Blaenavon in 1950 from the timber yard. At this time the pit was st
wound by an 1880 Fowler Steam winder with flat rope

Blaenavon Collieries, 1947-80			
Colliery		Persons employed Below ground	Above ground
1947	Big Pit	661	136
1958	Big Pit	908	151
1979	Big Pit	180	57
1980	Big Pit Closed	173	54
1947	Kay's Slope & Milfraen	281	69
1947	Garn Slope	541	137
1958	Garn Slope & Kay's Slope	547	126
1966	Garn Slope & Kay's Slope.	Closed	Closed

In 1973, coal winding at Big Pit ceased. A new drift had been driven near the washery enabling all coal to e raised, washed and blended on one site. From the te 1960s, all production was concentrated in the Garw eam. The maximum thickness of the Garw was 2ft 6in., s minimum 2ft 2in.

Until it closed in 1980, Blaenavon had some of the ldest workings in South Wales. Its drainage system was nique: it incorporated the Forge Level, Wood's Level and ear's Slope, all of them dating back to 1830 and before, hile the Engine Pit Level (c. 1810) was also retained as 1 emergency exit.

Today this complex comprises a UNESCO World Heritage Site; with a museum based upon the iron works and g Pit, enabling the heritage of iron and coal mining in outh Wales to be passed on to future generations.

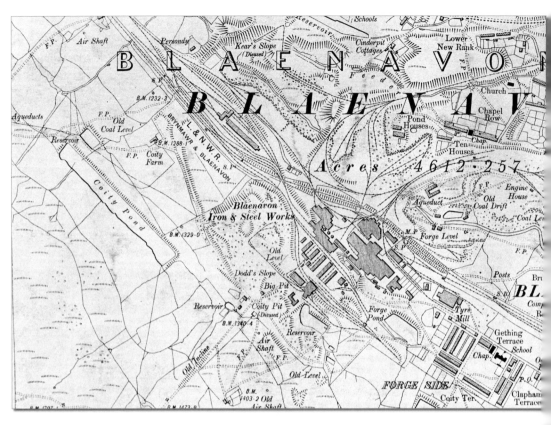

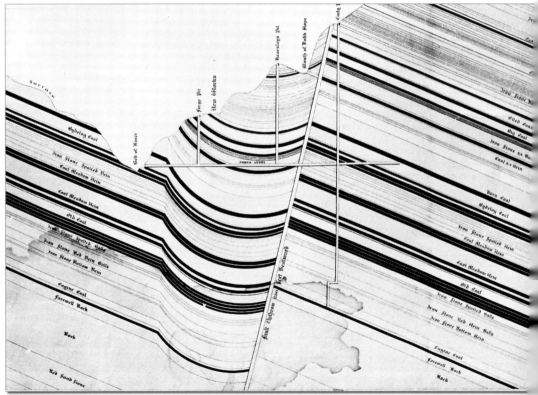

Above: General view of the Washery with the Garn Tips in background

Below: The manager talking to a deputy in the yard, 1975

The Engine Pit Level driven around 1810. This level was one of the oldest surviving mines in the Blaenavon complex and was kept as an emergency exit until 1979

Above: A brick lined level in the Blaenavon complex, probably the Forge Level, taken in 1975

Left: New roadway driven from the drift entrance with conveyor belt carrying coal from the Garw seam, 1978

Above: The abandoned pit bottom in 1975

Below: Bill Gunter, the Big Pit safety officer, on the G11 Face in 1979

Left: A plough on the G11 face, February 1979. This was the Garw seam, and was 28in. thick. It was the last seam to be worked in Big Pit

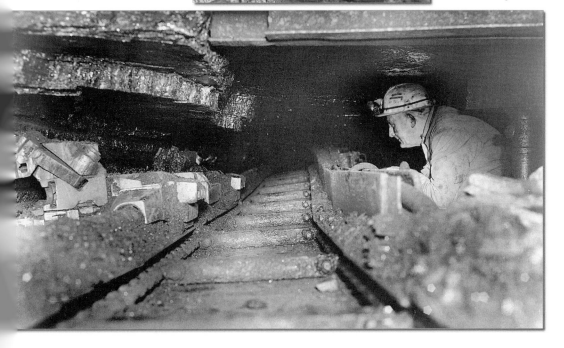

Above: A pit pony returning to Big Pit stable in 1968 after working in oneof the many levels in the complex

Above: *Nora* an Andrew Barclay locomotive in 1973 working in the yard of the original Blaenavon Iron Works. This line was used as the land sale yard

Above: The tail gate on G11 face, the Garw seam, at this time the seam section was around 2ft 4in

Above: The last day for Glyn Morgan, the final NCB manager, 28 November 1980

Left: Bill Gunter standing at the archway to Dick Kear's Slope, driven around 1820

Above: The Garn tips in winter

Right: Engine Pit Level with decayed timbering, used as a emergency exit until 1979

The River Arch Level driven some-time before 1840 and still in use today

Above: The original entrance to Woods level now partially flooded. Since a waste tip in the vicinity of the entrance extended across the valley, the entrance was continuall extended by adding steel rings. The River Arch level had to be extended in the same fashion

Left: A mine official examining a section of a cage of a water balance machine, near the bottom of the Forge Pit 1975

A fly wheel from a large steam haulage engine, used to support the pack wall Engine Pit 1975-6

BLAENAVON IRON WORKS AND EARLY MINING

Any publication on the South Wales Coalfield must contain a section on the iron industry. Had it not been for the presence of coal and iron-ore deposits, there would have been no South Wales iron industry. Although the there were many early charcoal furnaces scattered across the valleys, they had little impact on the landscape. It was the establishment of the larger coke-fired furnaces which was responsible for the establishment of the many iron towns like Blaenavon, Nantyglo, Merthyr Tydfil, and Dowlais and many others; these towns were established along the heads of the valleys where there were vast reserves of coking coals, iron-ore and limestone. The deposits of Pennant sandstone was also available as building material.

The Blaenavon iron works with its ancillary buildings and its workers' housing is the most complete of all Iron-Works sites in Great Britain, and certainly deserves its World Heritage Site status. Fortunately I saw and recorded the site in the late 60s and early 70s, when the furnaces stood out in a sea of rubble and broken stonework. Stack Square had lost most of its slates and some of the roof timbers had disappeared for firewood in one of the early miners' strikes. Regrettably I never recorded housing like Bunkers Row, but I did capture on film the Black Ranks

Above: The Blaenavon Iron Works in 1801 from Archdeacon William Coxe's book *An Historical Tour through Monmouthshire*. This plate shows the first three furnaces to be built, it is highly likely that the two round stacks between furnaces 1 and 2 are the chimneys of the Boulton and Watt blowing engine which was installed 1800. Furnaces 4 and 5 were later built against the rock face to the right of the furnaces. The most interesting feature is the archway of the Engine Coal Level, on the extreme right of the plate, which was clearly at work in 1801 (officially Fairmont Terrace) and Garn Terrace complete with chapel.

The working of coal at Blaenavon certainly predated the present iron-works. In 1775 William Tanner and Mary Gunter were granted a lease to work coal. These early workings would have been situated on or close to the outcrop areas, and may have been worked on the patch work system. These early coal works would have mainly supplied coal for lime-burning, blacksmiths and domestic use.

The early workings were patch works, followed by levels on the outcrops, some working coal but some clearly worked iron-ore. The Engine Pit Shaft was thought to be the first shaft to be sunk at Blaenavon.

It was in 1789 that a lease was granted by the Earl of Abergavenny to Thomas Hill of Stafford and his associates Thomas Hopkins and Benjamin Pratt, for an iron works for which coke was to be fuel.

New information now suggests that a primitive type of iron works running on charcoal existed at Blaenavon before the works commenced by Hill, Hopkins and Pratt. Whether the early works stood on the present site is not clear. It is stated that in 1786 the works were in operation again after some degree of stoppage owing to the exhaustion of the wood supplies in the vicinity.

A close examination of the maps and plans and early plates of Blaenavon raises more questions than it answers; the Boulton and Watt papers tell us that a steam blowing engine with a 40 in cylinder and 8 ft stroke was installed in 1800 with a cast iron beam. How were the furnaces blown from 1789 until around 1800? Was water power used for blowing, or was there an earlier steam powered blowing engine? The feeder situated just to the west of furnace No.3 is ideally placed for driving a water wheel or wheels. It is possible that a structure shown between furnaces No.1 and 2, on the 1801 engraving in Coxe's tour of Monmouthshire is the Boulton and Watt blowing engine installed in 1800. It certainly shows two chimnies.

Two mines are shown on page 43, an undated plan certainly made before the 1819 map of Blaenavon, on which two additional furnaces are shown. The Engine Coal Level which is shown to be of considerable size must have been driven prior to 1790 or even before. It could be that structure shown the right hand of Coxe's illustration is the entrance of the Engine Coal Level. Is the level situated behind and along side furnaces No.1 and 2, the mine mentioned by Coxe as being no less than three quarters of a mile in length?

Clearly there is still much to be learnt about the Blaenavon works in its early days.

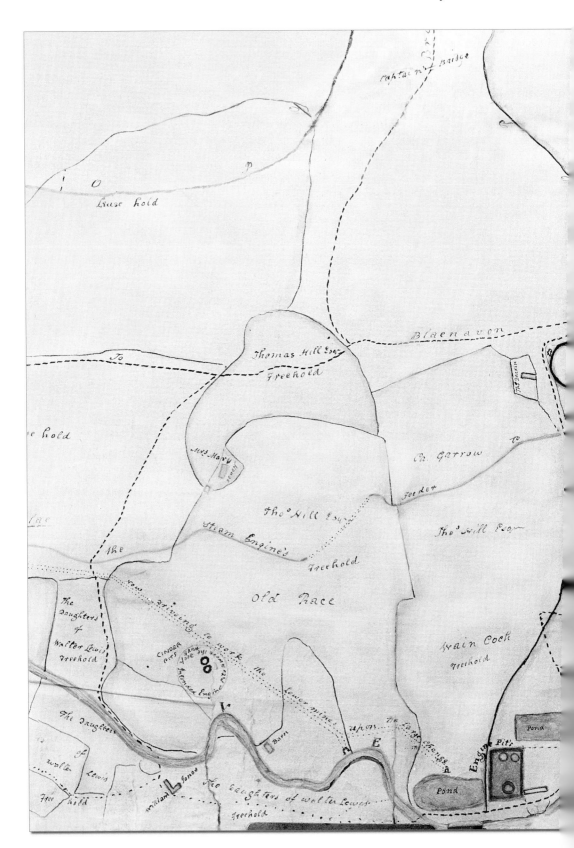

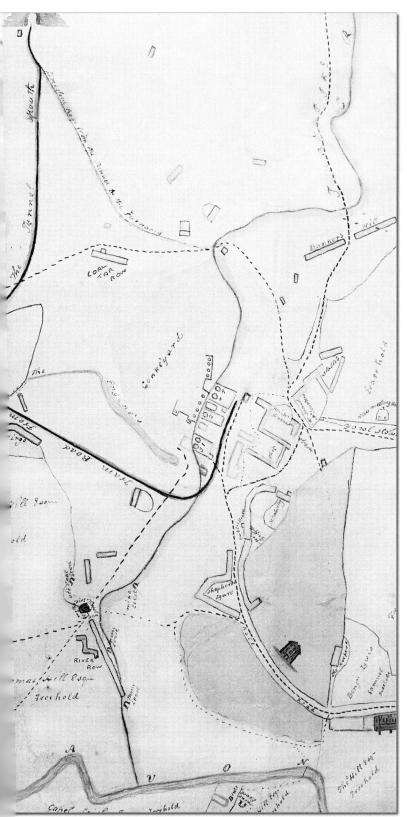

A map of the Blaenavon area and Iron Works by Thomas Deakin dated 1819. This interesting map shows the site of the intended Engine pits to work the deep coal, later known as the Cinder Pits. Note the Engine pit with what appears to be three shafts and two ponds, which may have been for a water wheels driving a pump on the engine shaft and water driven winding engine. The eastern section of this map covering the iron-works has been reproduced as a separate plate to show the interesting detail. Note that there are now five furnaces in production and the calcining kilns are situated behind the furnaces with the coke yard well to the north of the calcining kilns. Unfortunately this map does not show the complex of tramways carrying coal and iron-ore to the coke yard and calcining kilns. These missing tramways are clearly shown on the 1821 map in detail. The main tramway which carried pig-iron to the Brecknock and Abergavenny Canal through the Pwll Du Tunnel from the furnaces is shown as "The Tramroad from the Furnaces"

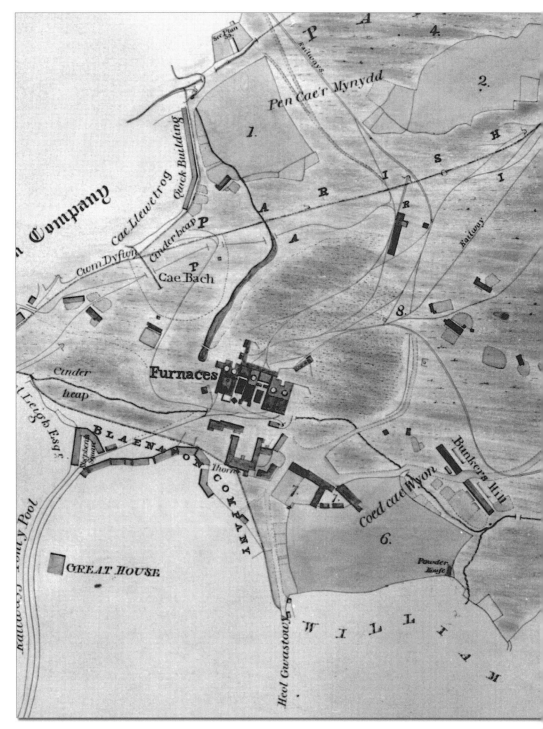

A map entitled *Blaenavon Iron Works in the Liberty in the Parishes of Llanover and Llanwenarth* by David Davies 1821. This map is interesting because of the large number of levels served by tramways operating in 1821. Many of these levels were producing 'mine' (iron ore) as well as coal

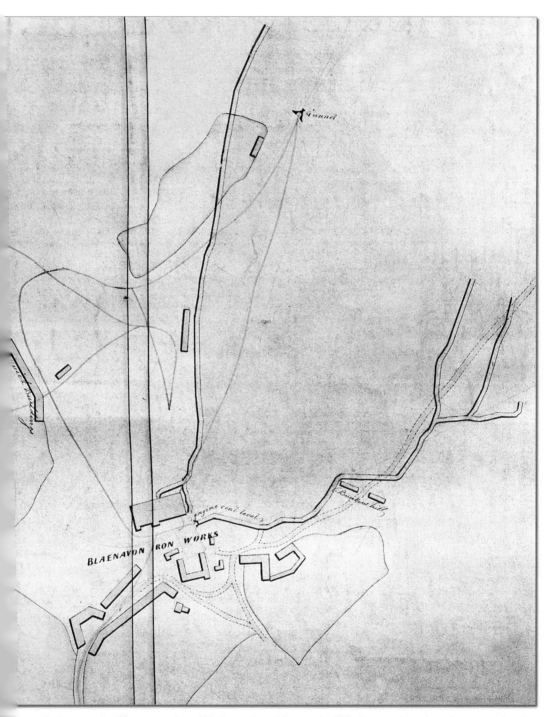

...lan of mines at the Blaenavon Iron Works undated but early. This interesting plan shows two levels, ... known as the Engine Coal Level and situated to the north east of Stack Square. A second mine is ...ated behind and along side the furnace No. 2. Furnaces No. 4 and 5 have not yet been built. The ...gine Coal Level is also shown on the 1821 map of Blaenavon, with a tramway. (see pp40/41)

Above: The surface of the Engine Pit in 1974 with its capped shaft and the remains of an early pumping arrangement

Right: The lower section of the shaft of the Engine Pit in 1975. Note the deposits of tar running down the walls of the shaft

bove: Bill Gunter the NCB Safety Officer at Big Pit, at the entrance to the Engine Level which led to ne Engine Pit shaft. This level was abandoned when Big Pit was closed by the NCB

ght: The River Arch
el which is thought to
the level shown on
Thomas Deakin map
1819 just west of the
gine pits

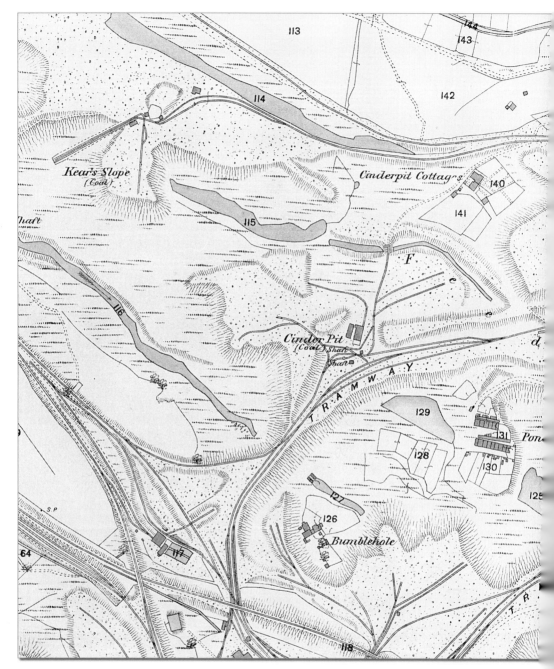

O. S. Map of 1882 showing the position of the early mines, Kear's Slope is situated to the North-W of the Cinder Pits. The date of the sinking of Dick Kear's Slope is not known, but was some time af 1830

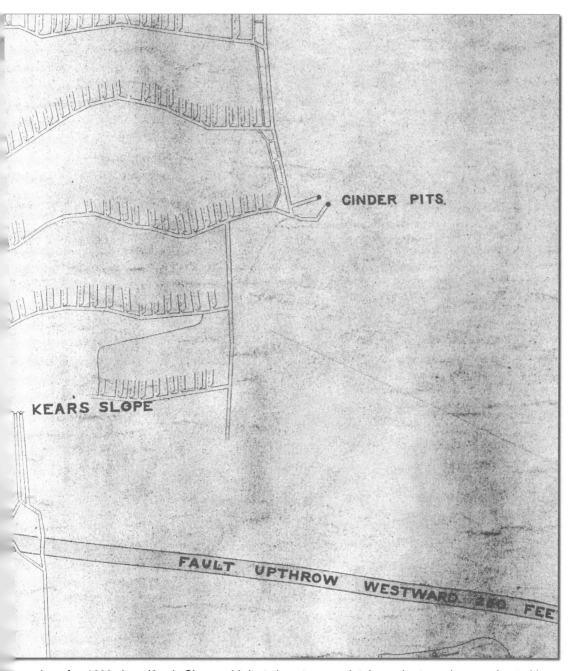

CINDER PITS.

KEARS SLOPE

FAULT UPTHROW WESTWARD 250 FEE

ne plan of c. 1890 show Kear's Slope, with its twin entrances, intake and return airways, situated just
st of the Cinder Pits

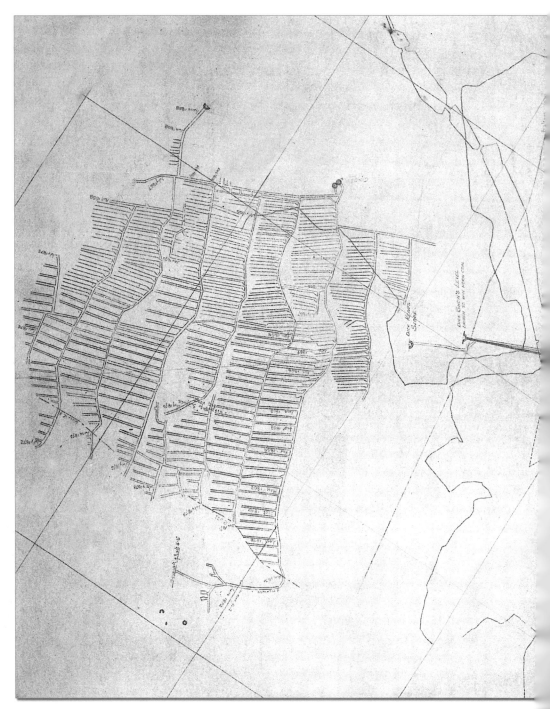

An earlier mine plan (date unknown), which shows the mine then known as Dick Kear's Slope with single inlet. The Horn Coal has been worked with the extensive workings ranging from 1866 to 18 Note the entrance to Dick Shon's level which is situated over Dick Kears Slope and is also intenc to work the Horn Coal

A mine plan showing stalls in the Black Pins Level in the 1870s, these workings are arranged along the strike so that the main roads are relatively level to accommodate horse haulage to the drifts where mechanical haulage was placed to haul up dip

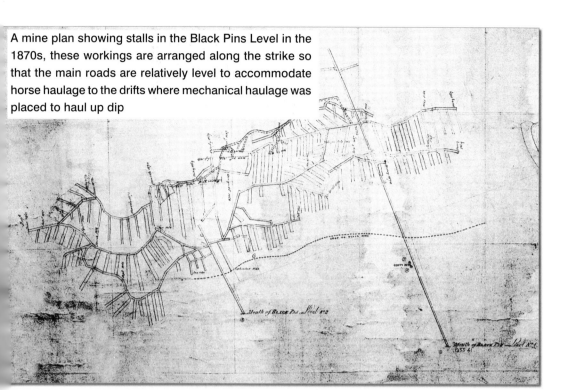

⊃king inbye from the stone lined entrance of Dick Kear's Slope. There were two entrances to Kear's ⊃e – an intake and a return; this roadway is thought to be the intake

Above: Looking back up the return road of Kear's Slope with plateway and early tram wheels ly around. The ventilation furnace was most likely situated further into the mine but is not shown on m plans. Taken in 1977-78

Above: Furnaces surrounded by fallen masonary, 1965

Right: Bell pits to the north of the furnaces, it is not clear whether workings are for coal or iron ore, the former are the most likely. these workings are possibly the workings shown on the right hand side of Coxe's engraving of 1801

Stack Square, Blaenavon, built prior to 1799 by the Blaenavon Iron & Coal Co. this photograph was taken in the late 1960s. This property had been previously owned by the National Coal Board. According to Commissioner Tremenheer writing, in 1850, Stack Square had no toilets. In fact he claims that," there was not a single W. C. to the whole of the cottages of the works". Note the brick outside toilets on the extreme left of the photograph, which served the whole of Stack Square, and probably dated from the early years of the 20th century

...e corner dwelling of Stack Square in 1968 with the balance tower in background. This housing has ...le of the Welsh style of construction and shows more of a Midland influence with its single ring brick ...ches over the windows and doors

The Balance Tower in 1973. This structure was built by the Kennards sometime after 1836

Above: Garn Terrace, Garn-yr-erw before the demolition of the chapel and removal of the Garn Tips. This housing is shown on the first edition of the O.S. Map and was certainly built before 1880

Above: Fairmont Terrace, Garn-yr-erw. This distinctive housing with its walls covered in pitch, and some houses with stable type doors were demolished soon after the photographs were taken in the 1970s. How draughty were these dwellings with their stable doors?

General view of Fairmont Terrace, also known as the Black Ranks, showing the thick covering of pitch to repel the elements which are severe at a height of 1,280 feet. This housing is not shown on the c. 1880 map, but is shown on 1900 edition. The housing was built by the Blaenavon Company and was later owned by the National Coal Board; it no longer exists

The old Blaenavon landscape before Fairmont Terrace and the Garn Tips were removed

Above: The washery tip in 1975; this tip was removed and would have enhanced the landscape of the World Heritage Site

Right: The tapping arch of the No.2 furnace, the best preserved furnace prior to restoration

ove: It is said that the brick building may have been the building in which the early work on the
ssemer Converter was carried out

posite page: The casting houses and furnaces of the Blaenavon works in the 1960s

ABERTILLERY NEW MINE
(FORMERLY ROSE HEYWORTH COLLIERY)
MONMOUTHSHIRE

Originally known as Rose Heyworth Colliery, it was sunk by the South Wales Colliery Co in 1872, and as the colliery appears in the Inspectors' list of mines in 1873, coal must have been raised by that date. By 1888 the colliery had been taken over by Lancasters' Steam Coa Collieries Ltd.. who then worked the colliery until nationalisation in 1947.

For many years Rose Heyworth Colliery was also connected to the South Griffin Colliery for pumping and ventilation, Rose Heyworth being the downcast and South Griffin No.3 the upcast; there was also a connection to Cwmtillery, with part of the Rose Heyworth working being ventilated by Cwmtillery.

The colliery had an attractive lattice headframe, and was originally wound by steam power electric winding replaced the steam power in the 1950s when a £3 million scheme was un dertaken. At the same time a new drift mine was driven to integrate Abertillery New Mine and Cwmtillery and raise coal from both pits. Coal from Blaenserchan Colliery was also transporte underground and brought up the Abertillery drift to the central washery and coal preparatio plant at the Abertillery New Mine.

This colliery used rail guides, as the shaft was not true and had a severe twist near the p bottom, so rope guides would not have worked.

By the late 1970s the workings were spread out over an area of over eight square mile lying to the north of two major faults, which separated the take from Blaenserchan and Blaenavo to the north. The complex had 31 miles of underground roadway, 11 miles of which were high-speed belt conveyors.

£100,000 was also spent on a new manriding installation, which was 3,000 metres i length, the longest system in the coalfield.

The colliery closed on the 9 October 1985, although Cwmtillery had closed in 1982.

Abertillery New Mine,
General view of
colliery yard 1978

Top of the Headframe, Abertillery New Mine

Abertillery New Mine

Pit bottom of Abertillery New Mine in 1977

Opposite page: Main trunk with conveyor in the Abertillery New Mine in 1978

Above: The entrance to the new drift at the New Mine with conveyor, 1978

Opposite page: Coal face in the New Mine, with chain hauled ranging drum shearer in 1978

Coal cutter at rest with haulage chain in foreground

BLAENDARE DRIFT MINE
BLAENDARE, PONTYPOOL, MONMOUTHSHIRE

This small mine had a complex history. The original date of opening is not known, but the list of abandoned mines of 1930 shows a Blaendare Mine at Cwmlicky working the Red vein and owned by the Ebbw Vale Steel Iron & Coal Co. I suspect that this is the Blaendare mine which was later owned by the Blaendare Co Ltd in 1936. It was registered at Pontypool, the concern being then owned and run by the Bythway family of Pontypool, who worked the Tillery Seam with 70 men underground and 25 on the surface.

The mine was taken into the National Coal Board in 1947 and employed 116 men underground and 33 on the surface. The mine then worked the Old Coal seam. At this time it had its own steam locomotive which was named *Blaendare*.

By 1950 the mine is shown as disused, but was then taken over by G. K. N. who worked the fireclay only until the late 1960s, when it became a licensed mine with a Mr Morris as manager working the Elled seam.

The mine closed in the early 1970s and the site was later the scene of opencast operations.

...aendare Mine. Entrance to drift, main intake. The return airway was situated to the south. Taken ...1969

Above: Original single inlet Sirocco fan, Blaendare mine 1969

Opposite page: Wooden trams standing outside the screens at Blaendare Mine in 1969

Empty trams at Blaendare Mine, this design had not changed in the last 100 years, these trams continuing in use until the mine closed in the 1970s

BLAENSERCHAN COLLIERY
NR PONTYPOOL, MONMOUTHSHIRE

Blaenserchan Colliery was sunk in 1890 by Partridge & Jones Ltd. The first shaft to be sunk was the present upcast shaft. Originally it was only sunk to the Old Coal, but later, in 1899, was deepened. The first 113 yards was elliptical in shape (16ft by 11ft) with the remainder being circular, 18 ft in diameter. The total depth is 362 yards; the depth to the Meadow vein being 351 yards. The Meadow vein coal was worked extensively from this shaft. The downcast shaft was sunk around 1915. It was 20 ft in diameter and had a depth of 354 yds. Prior to the second shaft been sunk, air was obtained from the Llanerch downcast shaft.

The main winding engine for many years was a Worsley Mesnes with 30 in cylinders and a 5 ft stroke; this engine could wind 700 tons per shift. The winding engine on the upcast shaft was an Uskside with 28 in cylinders, and a 4 1/2 ft stroke; this shaft was fitted with a single-deck cage, which held 16 men.

Ventilation was originally provided by a Walker steam driven fan, with a capacity of 200,000 cubic feet per minute; an electrically driven Sirocco fan served as a stand-by.

Blaenserchan Colliery. General view in 1969

Seams worked at Blaenserchan:

Elled
Big Vein
Threequarter
Black Vein
Meadow
Old Coal
The last seam to be worked was the Garw.

Until 1950 compressed air was the power used on the faces, but in the early 1950s the face machinery was electrified. In the Big Vein, undercutters were used which gave a 4 ft cut on a 60 yd face; it was expected to yield 80 tons per shift. Later, Panel C2 was 180 yds long and advanced on a 24 hour cycle, producing 240 tons a shift. By the late 1970s the plough had replaced the undercutter.

In 1969 coal winding ceased at Blaenserchan and for some years all coal was routed underground through Tirpentwys Colliery to Hafodyrynys Colliery for washing and despatch on British Rail.

In the final phase of working the take was contained by two major faults; one lying north-south. Between Blaenserchan and Llanhilleth Colliery, on the southern side of the take, was the extensive Trevethin Fault. The take was around four miles square, and the final workings in the Garw seam were 1,400 ft in depth.

In August 1977 all coal at Blaenserchan was re-routed underground to Abertillery New Mine but later all coal was raised at Marine Colliery.

Looking south across the valley in 1973

Left:
The colliery in 1969
before modernisation

Below:
The colliery after
modernisation,
photographed
in 1979

Above: The pit bottom in 1979 with supplies and a tram of waste

Above: Blaenserchan Colliery lamp room, 1978

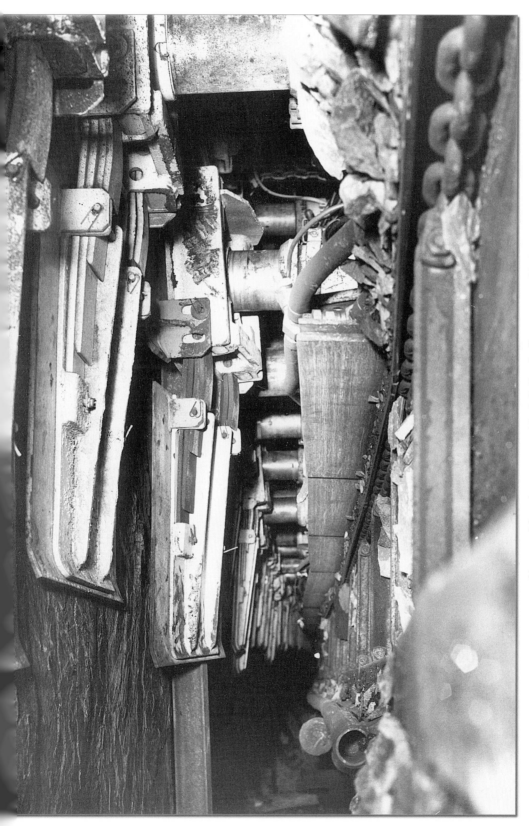

New coal face in process of installation in Garw seam, 1979

New haulage engine installed in 1979

GLYN PITS
PONTYPOOL, MONMOUTHSHIRE

The Glyn Pits were sunk around 1840-45 by Capel Hanbury Leigh. By the early 1860s the colliery was in the ownership of the Ebbw Vale Company which then worked the colliery until June 1909 when it passed into the hands of Crumlin Valley Collieries Ltd. The colliery then ceased working in 1932, but was retained as a pumping and ventilation unit for Hafodyrynys Colliery until the early 1960s.

The Glyn Pits with the Neath Abbey pumping engine in the late 1960s

On this colliery site are the sad remains of the magnificent vertical steam winding engine of c. 1840-45 and a double acting rotative beam engine made by the Neath Abbey Iron Works in 1845. These wonderful engines, which must be the oldest steam winding and pumping engines in their engine houses on their original site in South Wales, have been allowed by successive authorities to deteriorate to a point, where, if nothing is done very soon, the engines and their houses will collapse.

The winding arrangement was carried out in two shafts simultaneously, from a depth of 180 yards. The downcast shaft was 12 ft in diameter, with the upcast shaft 9 ft diameter. The maker of the vertical winding engine is not known, and is not included in the list of Neath Abbey Engines in Glamorgan Record Office, but there are certain features which are similar in both engines and I feel that the vertical winder could have been built at Neath Abbey, although it is not recorded. The rotative beam pump is listed in the Neath Abbey papers as being built in 1845.

The winding engine has a vertical cylinder, below floor level. It is double-acting, and operates vertically upwards, driving two 15 feet diameter flat rope drums positioned overhead. The valve gear was hand-operated, and the engine worked until 1932.

The beam engine is a vertical, double-acting single cylinder originally with a 30 in cylinder and 6 ft stoke. The engine was operated by steam at 50 psi. The condensing pump was operated from the main beam, and the piston rod is linked to an overhead oscillating beam which in turn is coupled to a crank shaft carrying a 17 ft diameter flywheel. Speed reduction was obtained through a pair of massive cast iron gear wheels with four inch pitch teeth.

The second motion shaft has a crank on the end coupled to a long horizontal wooden connecting rod, which actuates a bell crank lever system. The end of the lever carries the spear rod for operating the pumps in the shaft. Pumping was carried out in two stages from a depth of 186 yards, the pumps delivering up to 1,200 gallons per hour into a water course some 85 yards from the surface. The water then flowed through a level and emerged lower down in the valley.

The following seams of coal were raised from the Glyn Pits.

Name	depth in Yards	Ft	in
Soap Vein Coal	51	2	6
New Vein or Elled Coal	1	1	0
Big Coal	1	1	0
Red Vein or Three-Quarter Coal	1	0	8
Rock or Black Vein	2	2	0
Yard Vein Coal		2	6
John Williams Coal		1	0
Meadow Vein Coa	3	1	2
Old Coal	1	2	6
Rough Coal		1	10
Total	189	2	9

In addition, 5 veins of iron-ore were raised from the Glyn Pits prior to 1900.

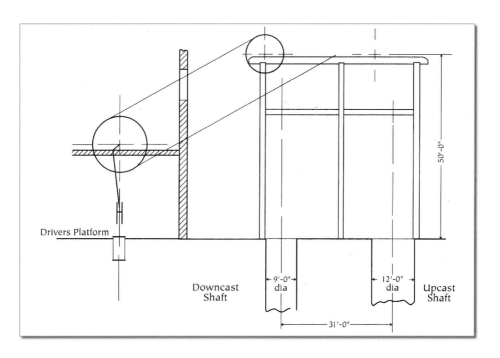

Drivers Platform

Downcast Shaft

← 9'-0" → dia

← 12'-0" dia

Upcast Shaft

50'-0"

← 31'-0" →

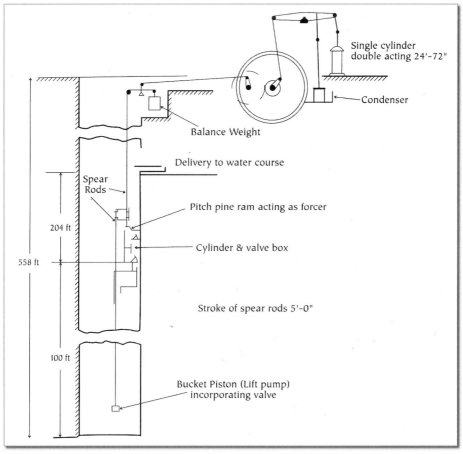

Single cylinder
double acting 24'-72"

Condenser

Balance Weight

Delivery to water course

Spear Rods

Pitch pine ram acting as forcer

Cylinder & valve box

Stroke of spear rods 5'-0"

Bucket Piston (Lift pump)
incorporating valve

558 ft

204 ft

100 ft

Left: The fine engine house for the vertical winding engine

Below: The Neath Abbey Pump. The fly wheel and gear wheels with a four inch pitch, which drove a long wooden connecting rod through a crank, now buried, which was coupled to a bell-crank level system; the end of the crank carries the spear rod for operating the pumps in the shaft

posite page: The magnificent tical steam winding engine in 1960s with the hand operated ve gear almost intact

above: The cylinder and piston rod of the pumping engine; note the interesting floor joist constructed with dove-tailed joints by the Neath Abbey Works

opposite page: The wooden connecting rod; the crank carried a large wooden balance box which contained early cranks and other cast iron objects

HAFODYRYNYS COLLIERY AND MINE
NR CRUMLIN, MONMOUTHSHIRE

The original Hafodyrynys mine appears in the Inspectors' List of Mines for the three years 1878-79-80; it was then owned by E. Jones. It was not until the Crumlin Valley Collieries started the sinking in 1911 that the name Hafodyrynys reappears; whether the new site was on or near the old Hafodyrynys mine is not known, but the sinking was completed by 1914.

In 1954-59 £5,500,000 was spent on linking Hafodyrynys new mine with the new Glyntillery drift, not to be confused with the Pontypool Glyntillery mine and Tirpentwys Colliery. Coal from Blaenserchan was also conveyed underground to Glyntillery to the washery and British Rail at Hafodyrynys mine.

Hafodyrynys mine closed in September 1966, Tirpentwys Colliery in September 1968, and Glyntillery in December 1975.

The following seams were worked at Hafodyrynys:
> Tillery or Red Ash Seam.
> Big Vein.
> Lower Threequarter.
> Black Vein.
> Meadow Vein.

Hafodyrynys Colliery. Looking east, the only remaining structure in 2001 was the round washery on the right of the picture

Hafodyrynys Colliery, with the Old Hafodyrynys Colliery on the left of the picture

Electric locomotive at entrance to drift in 1968

LLANHILLETH COLLIERY
MONMOUTHSHIRE

This colliery was situated in the Ebbw Valley just over half a mile north of the site of the Crumlin Viaduct, and consisted of three shafts. The No1 shaft was sunk by Walter Powell in 1860-70 to the Tillery seam. When the colliery was acquired by Partridge, Jones & Co Ltd in 1890, the No. 1 shaft was deepened, and the No. 2 shaft sunk to the Black Vein. Earlier workings at Llanhilleth are documented as early as 1802.

Llanhilleth Colliery had a fine beam engine built by Harvey of Hayle, Cornwall. It was installed on the No. 1 shaft and had a 70 in cylinder, with a 10 ft stoke, raising 400 gallons of water per minute. As with most Partridge & Jones Collieries, the winding engines were made by Uskside of Newport. The engine on the No.1 had 30 in cylinders, with a 5 ft stoke.

Llanhilleth Colliery around the turn of the century. The House coal shaft is on the right of the picture with the No.2 shaft behind the house coal pit. The No.1 shaft with its Cornish pump is situated to the west and is not shown

The No.1 pit was the upcast and was used in 1950 for ventilation only, the Cornish pumping engine had long been dismantled, although the engine house remained until the colliery was demolished around 1980. The No.1 shaft was elliptical and was 19 ft x 13 ft, depth 375 yds, to the Old Coal seam.

The No.2 shaft was the downcast and coal winding shaft, it was circular and 18 ft in diameter. The depth was 368 yds, with the coal raised from the Black Vein landing, at 318 yards.

The House Coal shaft was probably sunk to the Tillery seam and was unlined.

The main seams worked at Llanhilleth Colliery were the Big Vein, Three quarter, Black Vein, Meadow Vein and Old Coal. By 1950 the Black Vein in the area had been completely exhausted, and only the Big and the Meadow Veins were being worked .

Until 1949-50 the Old Coal was worked by heading and stalls, and the coal was raised at the No.1 Pit. After 1950 all coal was raised at the No.2 Pit; the Threequarter seam was opened up just after 1950, the old conveyors replaced, the haulage system was reorganised and a cycle of operations established.

The small lattice headframe on the House Coal Shaft in 1975

In 1950 the reserves of the Pit were stated to be:-

Big Vein	4,333,000
Threequarter	4,211,000
Black vein	Exhausted.
Meadow Vein	2,900,000
Old Coal	4,670,000
Total	16,670,000

Ventilation was provided by a steam driven Walker Fan, 24 ft in diameter, with a capacity of 50,000 cu. ft. per min, with a 4 1/2 in water gauge.

The pumping in 1950 was from the bottom of No1 Pit by means of two Pulsometer pumps, with a capacity of 60,000 gallons per hour, each pump averaging 400,000 gallons per day.

The Colliery was closed on the 22 March 1969.

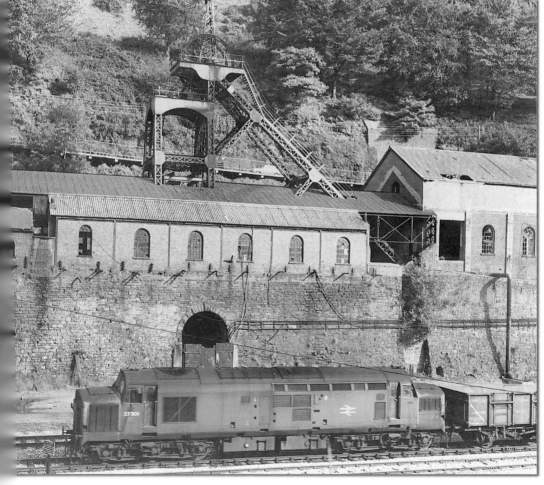

nhilleth Colliery: the No.2 shaft with a British Rail 37 Class locomotive, heading for the Ebbw e Works

The fine lattice headframe on the No.2 shaft, Llanhilleth Colliery 1975

The remains of the Cornish engine house on the No.1 shaft at Llanhilleth in 1974. The house held the large Cornish pump made by Harvey of Hayle, the engine had a 70 in cylinder, 10 ft stroke. This engine raised 400 gallons per minute in three lifts

MARINE COLLIERY
EBBW VALE, MONMOUTH

The Ebbw Vale Steel, Iron and Coal Company Limited commenced the sinking of the Marine shafts in 1887; the shafts were completed in 1893. The downcast shaft was 18ft in diameter and 1,254ft in depth. The upcast shaft was also 18ft in diameter and 1,242ft in depth, which included the sump. The two wrought iron headframes were constructed by Goddard, Massey & Warner of Nottingham.

The original winding engines were made by Nasmyth, Wilson and Co. of Patricroft, in 1890. The engine on the upcast shaft had two horizontal cylinders 41in. in diameter, a 6ft stroke and a drum of 18ft diameter. The engine on the downcast shaft had 36in. cylinders, 6ft stroke and a drum of 16ft. The engine on the upcast could raise 1,500 tons per day from the Old Coal seam.

The pumping engine, made by Hathorn Davey & Co. of Leeds, was placed under the winding engine on the downcast shaft. The engine and pumps could deal with 50,000 gallons of water per hour, when working at seven strokes per minute. Originally, ventilation was by a Schiele fan installed in 1891, driven by a compound steam engine; the fan had a diameter of 21ft, and could produce 120,000 cubic ft of air per minute. On 1 March 1927 the colliery suffered a disastrous explosion, when a firedamp ignition propagated by coal dust killed 52 men. In 1935 the Ebbw Vale Company sold all their collieries to Partridge, Jones & John Paton, Ltd., who then worked the colliery until Nationalisation in 1947.

In August 1982, a £2.5 million coal-winding improvement scheme was commissioned. The new high-speed pushbutton system of skip winding could raise over 500,000 tonnes of saleable coal in a year. In addition to the work in the shaft, a new coal handling plant was installed on the surface. The mine closed on 10 March 1989.

Opposite page: The unusual cast iron structure was made at the Risca Foundry Newport, and appears to have been made from rising mains. This interesting structure was replaced around 1980

A western class locomotive the *Western Consort* passing Marine Colliery in 1974

Rising mains and pump rods from the Hathorn Davey pump in 1980

Right: The removal of the Hathorn Davey engine's pump rod from the shaft. The rising mains were still in position in the brick lined shaft in the 1970s

Below: The original main pumping engine at Marine Colliery, built by Hathorn Davey of Leeds in 1893. The engine has a 36in. high pressure cylinder and a 68in. low pressure cylinder with a 10ft stoke. This engine cost £4,630 to install

Chainless haulage on the OC4s face on 15 October 1983

NORTH CELYNEN AND GRAIG FAWR COLLIERIES

The sinking of the North Pit of North Celynen Collieries was begun by the Newport Abercarn Black Vein Steam Coal Co in 1913; the first coal being raised in 1916. The North shaft, the downcast, was originally sunk to a depth of 427 yds and was 21 ft diameter, being further deepened in 1921. The total depth of the shaft in the 1950s was 515 yds. The South Pit was also 21ft in diameter and in the 1950s the full depth was 515 yards, but coal winding took place from the Three Quarter Vein landing at a depth of 426 yards.

In 1921 the colliery was acquired by the Ebbw Vale Iron & Coal Co Ltd, but was later sold to Partridge Jones & John Paton Ltd in 1937, which retained ownership until Vesting Date in 1947.

The colliery had worked continuously from 1915, working the Big Vein, Upper Threequarter, Lower Threequarter, Black Vein, Meadow Vein and Old Coal Vein.

North Celynen Colliery. General view in 1975

In the 1920s the workforce was around 1,500 men. A document in the possession of the author states:

" that the mine was large, but rather old fashioned, the shafts were over 500 yards deep, with single deck tandem cages. The winding engines were steam driven and rather old fashioned, as was most of the equipment on the surface. But the Graig Fawr Pit is very modern, and is an example of what can be achieved by good management, the road and ventilation were excellent. Graig Fawr Colliery was also using wood and steel adjustable props, most faces were longwall but one face was worked on the 'Barry' system with a tram road down the face."

After nationalisation the manpower figure at North Celynen and Graig Fawr fell, and in the era of fully mechanised faces and high speed conveyors, only 750 men were needed to produce 130,000 tonnes of coal. At Vesting Date, 90 per cent of the faces were hand cut and were worked by the longwall heading and stall method. Afterwards all the faces were converted to conveyor work, and machine cutting was adopted throughout the pit.

Both pits were originally equipped with steam winding engines as follows:

North Pit: Horizontal winder with 26 in cylinders, 40 in stroke, workings pressure 180 psi; the engine is said to have been built by Barclays.

South Pit: Horizontal winder with 28 in cylinders, 60 in stroke, working pressure 180 psi; the steam winders at North Celynen were removed and electrified in the late 1950s.

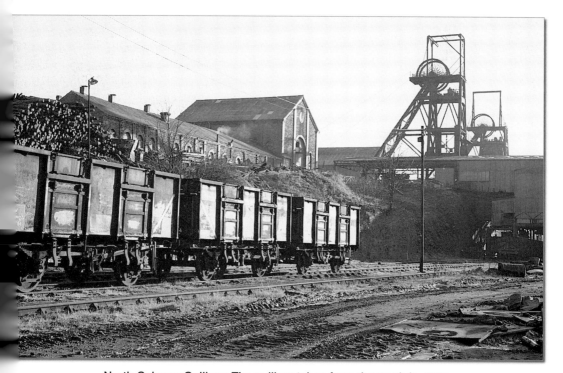

North Celynen Colliery: The colliery taken from the north in 1975

The fan engine was a Sirocco fan, 120 ins in diameter, driven by a 300 B.H.P motor. The capacity was 200,000 cu. ft per minute, with a 2.6 in water gauge.

The Graig Fawr or House Coal Shaft, which worked the Tillery seam, commenced working in 1924 and was abandoned in 1961.

By the late 1970s North Celynen worked an area of two and a half square miles, bounded on the south east by the 150 ft Pentwyn fault and the north by the 250 ft Britannia Overthrust.

The colliery was now linked to Oakdale and had over eight miles of underground roadways; of which two and a half miles were high-speed conveyors. Later the colliery was also linked in with Markham Colliery. This complex became the biggest unit in the South Wales Coalfield and new faces were planned to open in the Yard/Seven Feet, and in the early 1980s workings were in the Six Feet and Five Feet/Gellideg seams.

The colliery closed in 1986, when the men were transferred to Oakdale Colliery.

North Celynen Colliery: The pit bottom in 1978

Above: North Celynen Colliery Blacksmiths shop in 1975

Left: North Celynen Colliery. Graig Fawr Colliery also known as the House Coal Shaft, 1975

Above: North Celynen Colliery
Pumping station in 1975

Right: North Celynen Colliery
chain-hauled shearer on the coal
face, 1978

SIX BELLS COLLIERY
(ARRAEL GRIFFIN 4 AND 5)
SIX BELLS, MONMOUTH

John Lancaster & Co. commenced the sinking of Arrael Griffin in 1891; coal winding commenced several years later. There was a period of seven years from 1930 when the colliery was stopped due to lack of trade. In 1936 the colliery was taken over by Partridge, Jones & John Paton Ltd. who then worked it until Nationalisation. Vivian Colliery closed in 1958 and for several years the Vivian shaft became a downcast for Six Bells.

The early 1960s saw the electrification of the winding engines; in the early 1970s, the colliery was linked underground to Marine which then wound all the coal from Six Bells. In 1983 the only seam being worked was the Garw.

On 28 June 1960 an ignition of firedamp occurred at about 10.45 a.m. near the 0.10 face in the W district of the Old Coal seam. The coal dust was ignited and the explosion spread through the district, killing 45 of the 48 men working there at the time. The public enquiry, which was held later, felt that the firedamp could have been ignited by an incendiary spark caused by a fall of quartzitic stone on to a steel canopy.

Seams worked
at Six Bells

Elled
Big Vein
Threequarter
Black Vein
Meadow Vein
Old Coal; Garw.

...ght: A Torque ...nsion track-mounted ...draulic drilling rig. ...is drill advanced ...unnel in the Garw ...k by 51ft a week, ...re than double the ...evious best. The ...chine would drill a ...hole in hard rock ...ne minute and 20 ...conds, compared ...h 30 minutes using a ...d held drill

Above: Six Bells in 1979

Opposite page: The tub circuit in 1976

Above: Full tubs near the pit bottom. Soon after this was taken, all coal was carried underground to Marine Colliery

Left: Hand packed gob plough face in the Garw seam

Opposite page: Overman on chock face in the Garw seam, 1978

TIRPENTWYS COLLIERY
PONTYPOOL, MONMOUTH

The sinking of the two shafts at Tirpentwys Colliery commenced around 1878 and the first coal was raised in 1881 as the colliery first appears in the Inspectors' List of Mines for that year. The first owners were Darby & Norris, but by 1884 Tirpentwys was owned by the Tirpentwys Colliery Co. Several years later the Tirpentwys Black Vein Steam Coal & Coke Co. was formed and this concern continued to operate the colliery until Nationalisation in 1947.

The downcast shaft was 16ft in diameter, depth 1,326ft. The upcast shaft was 14ft in diameter, depth 1,278ft.

The original colliery winding engine was of the vertical type and was made by Daglish & Co with two vertical cylinders 40 in. in diameter, and a stroke of 6 ft.

Seams worked at Tirpentwys Colliery: The Elled, Big Vein, Three Quarter Seam, Black Vein Seam, Meadow Vein and Old Coal seam.

The colliery ceased coaling in 1969, but the shafts and winders were retained for pumping and ventilation and, since coal from Blaenserchan Colliery was routed underground to Hafodyryny Colliery via Tirpentwys, for washing and dispatch on British Rail.

Right: Tirpentwys in 1975. The colliery closed in 1969, but was retained for pumping and ventilation. The fine vertical engine housed an electric winder by Wild & Co; the unusual headframe was designed to work with a large vertical steam winding engine

Opposite page: Engine house and fan of a Walker fan

electric three-throw pumps on the Tillery Landing

Opposite page: The pit bottom of the down cast shaft

Four Colliery Classics for your bookshelf

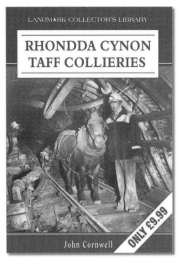

96pp/£9.99
Includes: Tower, Fernhill, Mardy, Tymawr/Gt Western, Lewis Merthyr, Bwllfa, Ferndale, Cymmer, Cwm/Coedely, Aberaman, Lady Windsor/Abercynon

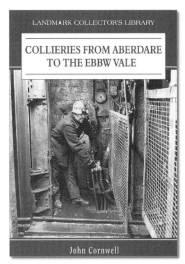

96pp/£9.99
Includes: Bargoed, Bedwas, Britannia, Deep Duffryn, Deep Navigation, Elliot, Fernhill, Llanover, Markham, Merthyr Vale, Nantgarw/Windsor, Nixon's Navigation, Oakdale, Penalta, Penrikiber, S. Celynen, Taff Merthyr, Trelewis, Ty Trist

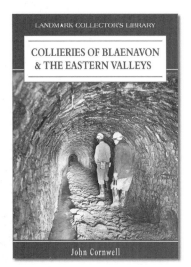

96pp/£9.99
Includes: Blaenavon (Big Pit, Iron Works & Early Mines), Abertillery, Blaenserchan, Blaendare, Glyn Pits, Hafodrynys, Llanhilleth, Marine, N. Celynen, Six Bells, Terpentwys

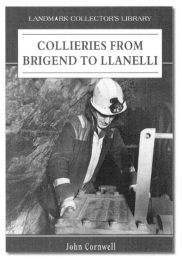

112pp/£9.99
Includes: Aberpergwm, Abernant, Ammanford, Betws, Blaengwrach, Brynlliw/Morlais, Cefn Coed/Blaenant, Clydach Merthyr, Coegnant, Cwmgwili and Lindsey, Cynheidre, Garw & Ffaldau, Glyntillery, Craig Merthyr, Main, Scot's Pit, Treforgan, Wyndham/Western, S. Wales Coking Works

The Oaks, Moor Farm Road West, Ashbourne, DE6 1HD
Tel: (01335) 347349 Fax: (01335) 347303
email: landmark@clara.net